FINANCIAL MANAGEMENT

Tackling the Matriarchy's Bullsh*t to Become an Expert with Money and Create a Life You Enjoy

Profitable Man

Table of Contents

CHAPTER ONE

Breaking Down Matriarchal Money Myths: Unveiling Financial Realities

In the realm of personal finance, societal narratives often perpetuate certain myths and misconceptions that influence individuals' beliefs and behaviors, shaping their financial destinies. The notion of a matriarchal influence on financial decisions is one such area that deserves closer examination. In the chapter titled "Breaking Down Matriarchal Money Myths: Unveiling Financial Realities," we embark on a journey to dissect common misconceptions, challenge stereotypes, and shed light on the complex dynamics that surround gender and money.

Deconstructing Stereotypes:

The first section of this chapter delves into the prevalent stereotypes associated with the intersection of gender and finance. Stereotypes such as men being inherently better at handling money or women being more risk-averse are explored and critically analyzed. By challenging these assumptions, readers are encouraged to question the validity of such stereotypes and recognize the diversity of financial skills and preferences within both genders.

Understanding the Impact of Societal Expectations:

This section delves into the societal expectations placed on individuals based on their gender, particularly in the context of financial responsibilities. Exploring how traditional gender roles may influence financial decision-making, the chapter encourages readers to recognize and confront societal norms that might limit their financial potential. By understanding these expectations, individuals can begin to break free from imposed constraints and make more informed financial choices.

The Role of Education and Empowerment:

A key aspect of dismantling matriarchal money myths involves emphasizing the importance of financial education and empowerment. This section discusses the significance of equipping individuals, regardless of gender, with the necessary knowledge and skills to navigate the complexities of personal finance. By promoting financial literacy, readers can gain confidence in making informed decisions, breaking free from outdated assumptions about gender and financial acumen.

Navigating Cultural and Historical Contexts:

This section explores how cultural and historical contexts contribute to the perpetuation of matriarchal money myths. By examining the historical roots of gender roles in financial matters, readers gain insights into the evolution of these narratives and how they continue to impact contemporary financial behaviors. Understanding the broader context allows individuals to approach their financial journeys with a more nuanced perspective.

Fostering Inclusive Financial Dialogue:

The final section of the chapter advocates for fostering open and inclusive conversations about money. Breaking down matriarchal money myths involves creating a space where individuals of all genders can share their experiences, challenges, and successes in the realm of personal finance. By promoting dialogue, this chapter aims to contribute to a cultural shift towards a more equitable and inclusive approach to financial discussions.

Conclusion:

"Breaking Down Matriarchal Money Myths: Unveiling Financial Realities" serves as a critical exploration of the misconceptions surrounding gender and finance. By challenging stereotypes, understanding societal expectations, promoting education, navigating cultural contexts, and fostering inclusive dialogue, this chapter empowers individuals to embrace financial independence free from the constraints of outdated and limiting beliefs.

Examining Gender Disparities:

The chapter commences by delving into empirical evidence and research that highlight existing gender disparities in the financial realm. From the gender pay gap to disparities in investment patterns, readers are provided with a comprehensive overview of how gender imbalances manifest across various financial aspects. By establishing a foundation rooted in data, the chapter sets the stage for a nuanced examination of gender dynamics in finance.

Unpacking the Gender Pay Gap:

A central focus of this section is the exploration of the gender pay gap and its ramifications on financial well-being. By dissecting the factors contributing to this gap, such as occupational segregation and systemic biases, readers gain insights into the challenges faced by individuals, particularly women, in achieving financial equality. Understanding the economic implications of the gender pay gap is crucial for fostering conversations about fair compensation and financial empowerment.

Gendered Perspectives on Investment:

This segment scrutinizes how gender influences investment behaviors and decision-making processes. Whether it be risk tolerance, investment styles, or access to financial resources, the chapter elucidates how societal expectations and stereotypes can shape individuals' approaches to investing. By acknowledging and addressing these gendered perspectives, readers are encouraged to diversify their understanding of investment strategies and consider the unique financial goals and challenges faced by different genders.

The Impact of Cultural Norms:

Gender dynamics in finance are intricately woven into the fabric of cultural norms and expectations. This section explores how societal expectations, influenced by cultural norms, can shape financial roles and responsibilities assigned to individuals based on their gender. By recognizing the influence of culture, readers are empowered to challenge and redefine traditional gender roles in finance, fostering a more inclusive and equitable financial landscape.

Strategies for Gender-Inclusive Financial Practices:

The final section of the chapter focuses on proactive strategies to create a more gender-inclusive financial environment. From promoting financial literacy programs that cater to diverse needs to advocating for workplace policies that address gender disparities, the chapter offers practical insights and recommendations for individuals, institutions, and policymakers alike. By implementing these strategies, readers can actively contribute to dismantling gender barriers in finance.

"Understanding Gender Dynamics in Finance: Unveiling Financial Realities" serves as a comprehensive exploration of the intricate relationship between gender and finance. By examining disparities, unpacking the gender pay gap, scrutinizing investment perspectives, acknowledging cultural influences, and proposing inclusive strategies, this chapter aims to foster a deeper understanding of gender dynamics in the financial realm and inspire meaningful action toward a more equitable and inclusive financial future.

Debunking Stereotypes: Men and Money - Unveiling Financial Realities

The Myth of Financial Invulnerability:

One prevalent stereotype surrounding men and money is the perception of financial invulnerability. This section explores the misconception that men are inherently more adept at navigating financial challenges and are less susceptible to economic hardships. By delving into real-world examples and acknowledging the impact of societal expectations, readers are prompted to challenge the notion that men are immune to financial struggles.

Breaking Down the Provider Stereotype:

Another stereotype addressed in this chapter is the traditional notion of men as primary financial providers for their families. The discussion delves into the evolving dynamics of family structures and challenges the assumption that men bear the sole responsibility for financial provision. By recognizing the diversity of family models and financial contributions, readers are encouraged to question and redefine their perceptions of men's roles in the context of financial support.

Addressing Risk-Taking and Investing:

This section explores stereotypes related to men's risk-taking behavior in financial matters, particularly in the context of investing. The chapter examines how societal expectations may influence the perception that men are more inclined to take risks in investment decisions. By providing a balanced perspective on risk tolerance and investment strategies, readers gain insights into the individualized nature of financial decision-making, challenging stereotypes that oversimplify men's approaches to investments.

Emotional Intelligence in Financial Decision-Making:

Contrary to the stereotype that men are less emotionally involved in financial decisions, this segment delves into the importance of emotional intelligence in money management. By exploring how emotional factors, such as stress, confidence, and communication, impact financial choices, the chapter challenges the notion that men approach financial decisions solely from a rational standpoint. Understanding the emotional dimensions of financial decision-making contributes to a more holistic view of men's relationships with money.

Navigating Career and Financial Pressures:

The final section of the chapter addresses the societal pressures on men to prioritize career success and financial achievements. By examining the impact of these expectations on mental health and overall well-being, readers are encouraged to consider the broader implications of societal pressures on men's financial behaviors. The chapter promotes a more compassionate and understanding perspective, emphasizing the importance of a balanced approach to career and financial fulfillment.

Conclusion:

"Debunking Stereotypes: Men and Money - Unveiling Financial Realities" serves as a critical exploration of the stereotypes that influence perceptions of men's financial behaviors. By challenging assumptions related to financial invulnerability, provider roles, risk-taking, emotional intelligence, and career pressures, this chapter aims to foster a more nuanced understanding of how men navigate the complexities of personal finance. Through this nuanced lens, readers are encouraged to approach financial discussions with open-mindedness and reject oversimplified stereotypes that limit our understanding of diverse financial experiences.

CHAPTER TWO

Overcoming Limiting Beliefs About Financial Success: Mastering Money Mindset

Identifying Limiting Beliefs:

This section delves into the exploration of common limiting beliefs that individuals may hold about financial success. From notions of unworthiness or fear of abundance to deep-seated beliefs about money being inherently evil, the chapter encourages readers to introspect and recognize the subconscious barriers that may hinder their financial growth. By acknowledging these limiting beliefs, individuals can take the first step towards dismantling them and embracing a more positive money mindset.

The Influence of Childhood Programming:

Limiting beliefs about money often stem from childhood experiences and societal conditioning.

This segment explores the impact of childhood programming on shaping attitudes towards wealth, success, and abundance. By understanding the roots of these beliefs, readers can work towards reprogramming their mindset, freeing themselves from inherited constraints, and fostering a healthier relationship with financial success.

Cultivating a Growth Mindset:

The chapter emphasizes the importance of adopting a growth mindset in the realm of personal finance. Unlike a fixed mindset that sees financial abilities as innate traits, a growth mindset views them as skills that can be developed through learning and experience. By cultivating a growth mindset, individuals can approach financial challenges as opportunities for growth rather than insurmountable obstacles, paving the way for continuous improvement.

Rewriting Money Stories:

An integral aspect of mastering the money mindset involves rewriting personal narratives about money. This section guides readers through the process of reevaluating and reframing their stories, transforming negative narratives into empowering ones. By reshaping the way individuals think and talk about money, they can create a narrative that aligns with their financial goals, fostering a positive and forward-thinking mindset.

Embracing Abundance and Prosperity:

The final segment of the chapter encourages readers to shift their focus from scarcity to abundance. By recognizing and appreciating the abundance that surrounds them, individuals can develop a mindset that attracts prosperity. This involves practicing gratitude, visualizing success, and aligning thoughts and actions with a mindset of abundance. Embracing the belief that there is enough for everyone can be a transformative step towards achieving financial success.

"Overcoming Limiting Beliefs About Financial Success: Mastering Money Mindset" serves as a guide to liberate individuals from the constraints of limiting beliefs and cultivate a mindset conducive to financial success. By identifying and challenging limiting beliefs, understanding the influence of childhood programming, adopting a growth mindset, rewriting money stories, and embracing abundance, readers can embark on a journey towards a more positive and empowering relationship with money. This chapter underscores the profound impact of mindset on financial outcomes, urging individuals to master their money mindset as a foundational step towards achieving lasting financial success.

Cultivating a Positive Relationship with Money: Mastering Money Mindset

Understanding the Emotional Landscape of Money:

The journey begins with an examination of the emotional landscape associated with money. From joy and security to anxiety and guilt, money can evoke a range of emotions. This section encourages readers to reflect on their emotional responses to financial matters, recognizing how past experiences and societal influences may shape their current attitudes. Understanding the emotional dimensions of money sets the stage for cultivating a positive and balanced relationship.

Challenging Negative Associations:

Many individuals carry negative associations and beliefs about money, often stemming from cultural influences, family upbringing, or personal experiences. This part of the chapter delves into identifying and challenging these negative associations. By questioning ingrained beliefs that may hinder financial growth, readers can pave the way for a more constructive and positive mindset towards money.

Embracing Financial Self-Worth:

A positive money mindset is intricately tied to one's sense of self-worth. This section explores the concept of financial self-worth, emphasizing that individuals are not defined by their financial circumstances. By dissociating personal value from financial success or failure, readers can foster a positive self-image, empowering them to make financial decisions from a place of confidence and self-assurance.

Adopting Mindful Spending Habits:

Mindfulness plays a crucial role in cultivating a positive relationship with money. The chapter introduces the concept of mindful spending, encouraging individuals to approach their financial transactions with intention and awareness. By aligning spending habits with personal values and goals, readers can break free from impulsive or emotionally-driven financial decisions, fostering a positive and intentional approach to money management.

Building a Foundation of Financial Gratitude:

Gratitude is a transformative tool in cultivating a positive money mindset. This segment explores the practice of financial gratitude, wherein individuals consciously acknowledge and appreciate the resources and opportunities available to them. By shifting the focus from what is lacking to what is abundant, readers can instill a sense of contentment and positivity in their financial journey.

Navigating Financial Challenges with Resilience:

The final section of the chapter addresses the inevitability of financial challenges. Cultivating a positive relationship with money involves developing resilience in the face of setbacks. By viewing challenges as opportunities for growth and learning, individuals can maintain a positive mindset even in turbulent financial times. This resilience is a key component of long-term financial well-being.

"Cultivating a Positive Relationship with Money: Mastering Money Mindset" serves as a roadmap for individuals seeking to transform their relationship with money. By understanding the emotional landscape, challenging negative associations, embracing financial self-worth, adopting mindful spending habits, building a foundation of financial gratitude, and navigating challenges with resilience, readers can cultivate a positive money mindset. This chapter emphasizes that a healthy and positive relationship with money is not only achievable but also essential for achieving lasting financial well-being and fulfillment.

Reexamining Traditional Masculine Financial Roles:

The chapter opens with a critical examination of traditional masculine financial roles. Historically, men have been associated with the role of primary financial providers, often carrying the burden of societal expectations. This section encourages readers to question and reevaluate these traditional roles, recognizing that financial responsibilities can and should be shared in modern relationships. Shifting away from rigid gender roles allows for a more equitable distribution of financial responsibilities and fosters a healthier mindset towards financial well-being.

Embracing Financial Vulnerability:

Traditional masculinity often discourages vulnerability, even in the realm of finances. This part of the chapter explores the importance of embracing financial vulnerability as a means of fostering open communication and seeking support when needed. By acknowledging that everyone faces financial challenges, irrespective of gender, individuals can break free from the stigma associated with financial difficulties and approach their financial well-being with authenticity and openness.

Redefining Success Beyond Material Accumulation:

A significant aspect of shifting perspectives on masculinity and financial well-being involves redefining success beyond material accumulation. Traditional notions often tie a man's worth to his financial achievements and possessions. This section challenges readers to broaden their definition of success, incorporating aspects of personal fulfillment, well-being, and meaningful connections. By embracing a more holistic view of success, individuals can free themselves from the pressure to conform to narrow definitions of masculinity in the financial realm.

Encouraging Financial Literacy and Education:

Shifting perspectives on masculinity and financial well-being involves advocating for increased financial literacy and education for everyone, irrespective of gender. This segment explores the importance of equipping individuals with the knowledge and skills needed to make informed financial decisions. By promoting financial education, societies can empower individuals to navigate their financial journey with confidence, breaking free from the limitations imposed by outdated notions of masculinity.

Fostering Healthy Communication about Finances:

Communication is a cornerstone of healthy financial relationships. This section encourages individuals to engage in open and transparent communication about money matters. Shifting away from traditional stoic masculinity, where discussions about finances may be considered taboo, fosters a more collaborative and supportive approach to financial well-being. Honest conversations about financial goals, challenges, and expectations contribute to a positive and inclusive money mindset.

Celebrating Diverse Financial Narratives:

The final part of the chapter emphasizes the importance of celebrating diverse financial narratives. Every individual's financial journey is unique, shaped by various factors such as background, experiences, and aspirations. By acknowledging and celebrating this diversity, readers can appreciate that there is no one-size-fits-all approach to financial success. Shifting perspectives on masculinity involves recognizing and valuing the multitude of ways individuals can thrive financially.

Conclusion:

"Shifting Perspectives on Masculinity and Financial Well-being: Mastering Money Mindset" serves as a guide for individuals seeking to liberate themselves from the constraints of traditional gender roles in the realm of personal finance. By reexamining traditional masculine financial roles, embracing financial vulnerability, redefining success, promoting financial literacy, fostering healthy communication, and celebrating diverse financial narratives, this chapter encourages a more inclusive and empowering approach to mastering the money mindset. It underscores the importance of embracing a mindset that values authenticity, communication, and flexibility, ultimately contributing to a more equitable and fulfilling financial future for all.

CHAPTER THREE

Building a Strong Foundation: Budgeting and Saving - Strategies for Financial Empowerment

Understanding the Importance of Budgeting:

The journey begins with a comprehensive understanding of budgeting as a fundamental tool for financial management. This section explores the concept of budgeting as a proactive and empowering practice, dispelling the misconception that it restricts financial freedom. By highlighting how budgeting serves as a roadmap for financial decisions, readers are encouraged to view it as a tool that brings clarity and control to their financial lives.

Creating a Realistic Budget:

This segment focuses on the practical steps involved in creating a realistic budget tailored to individual needs and goals. From tracking income and expenses to categorizing spending habits, readers are guided through the process of developing a budget that aligns with their financial objectives. The chapter emphasizes the importance of transparency and honesty during this process, setting the stage for effective financial planning.

Prioritizing Savings Goals:

Saving is a cornerstone of financial empowerment, providing a safety net for unexpected expenses and creating opportunities for future financial growth. This part of the chapter explores the significance of setting and prioritizing savings goals. Whether it's an emergency fund, a down payment for a home, or retirement savings, readers learn how to allocate their resources strategically to achieve both short-term and long-term financial objectives.

Implementing Effective Saving Strategies:

Building on the importance of savings, this section delves into actionable strategies for effective saving. From automated transfers to setting aside a percentage of income, readers are introduced to practical methods that facilitate consistent and sustainable savings habits. The chapter emphasizes the power of compounding and the impact of small, consistent contributions over time, reinforcing the idea that every saving effort, regardless of size, contributes to financial empowerment.

Navigating Challenges and Adjusting Strategies:

The financial landscape is dynamic, and unexpected challenges may arise. This part of the chapter addresses the importance of flexibility in financial planning. Readers learn how to navigate unexpected expenses, fluctuations in income, and other challenges by adjusting their budgeting and saving strategies accordingly. This adaptability is key to maintaining financial resilience and staying on track towards financial goals.

Integrating Financial Wellness into Everyday Life:

The final section of the chapter emphasizes the integration of financial wellness into everyday life. It encourages readers to view budgeting and saving not as temporary measures but as ongoing habits that contribute to a lifestyle of financial empowerment. By making financial wellness a consistent part of their routine, individuals can build a strong foundation that withstands the test of time.

Conclusion:

"Building a Strong Foundation: Budgeting and Saving - Strategies for Financial Empowerment" serves as a practical guide for individuals seeking to take control of their financial destinies. By understanding the importance of budgeting, creating realistic budgets, prioritizing savings goals, implementing effective saving strategies, navigating challenges, and integrating financial wellness into everyday life, readers are equipped with the tools and knowledge needed to establish a robust financial foundation. This chapter underscores that through disciplined budgeting and strategic saving, individuals can lay the groundwork for a financially empowered and secure future.

The Importance of Long-Term Vision:

At the core of investing for long-term wealth is the cultivation of a strategic and forward-thinking perspective. This section explores the significance of having a long-term vision when it comes to investments. By understanding that wealth-building is a gradual process, readers are encouraged to set realistic goals, develop patience, and align their investments with their overarching financial objectives.

Diversification and Risk Management:

Diversification is a key principle discussed in this chapter, emphasizing the importance of spreading investments across different asset classes to mitigate risks. Readers are guided through the concept of risk management, understanding how diversifying their investment portfolio can contribute to minimizing the impact of market fluctuations. This section underscores the need for a well-balanced and diversified approach to building long-term wealth.

The Power of Compounding:

One of the most potent tools in long-term wealth creation is compounding. This part of the chapter explores the exponential growth that occurs when earnings from investments generate additional returns over time. Readers gain insights into harnessing the power of compounding by making consistent contributions and reinvesting returns, ultimately accelerating the growth of their investment portfolios.

Strategic Asset Allocation:

Strategic asset allocation is a crucial strategy discussed in this section, highlighting the importance of aligning investments with individual risk tolerance, financial goals, and time horizons. Readers are guided through the process of determining the optimal mix of assets, such as stocks, bonds, and other investment vehicles, to create a well-balanced and personalized investment strategy that maximizes returns while minimizing risk.

Continuous Learning and Adaptation:

The financial landscape is dynamic, and this section underscores the necessity of continuous learning and adaptation in the realm of investing. Readers are encouraged to stay informed about market trends, economic developments, and changes in investment strategies. The ability to adapt to evolving financial climates empowers individuals to make informed decisions and optimize their investment portfolios for long-term wealth creation.

Tax-Efficient Investing:

Tax efficiency is a critical consideration in the pursuit of long-term wealth. This part of the chapter explores strategies for minimizing tax liabilities on investment gains, such as utilizing tax-advantaged accounts and understanding the tax implications of different investment vehicles. Readers gain insights into optimizing their investment strategy to maximize after-tax returns, thereby enhancing their overall financial empowerment.

Sustainable and Ethical Investing:

As societal awareness grows, the chapter also addresses the rising interest in sustainable and ethical investing. Readers are introduced to the concept of investing with environmental, social, and governance (ESG) considerations. Understanding how investments can align with personal values empowers individuals to make choices that not only yield financial returns but also contribute to positive social and environmental impacts.

"Investing for Long-Term Wealth: Strategies for Financial Empowerment" serves as a comprehensive guide for individuals seeking to build enduring financial security through strategic investment decisions. By emphasizing the importance of a long-term vision, diversification, the power of compounding, strategic asset allocation, continuous learning, tax-efficient investing, and considerations for sustainable and ethical investing, this chapter equips readers with the knowledge and tools to navigate the complex world of investments. By adopting these strategies, individuals can take significant steps toward achieving their long-term financial goals, fostering empowerment and resilience in the face of financial challenges.

Unpacking Matriarchal Expectations:

This section delves into the societal expectations placed on individuals based on matriarchal norms, exploring how they influence financial decision-making. From traditional roles in family finances to expectations about risk aversion and investment preferences, the chapter encourages readers to critically examine these expectations. By recognizing and understanding matriarchal influences, individuals can navigate them more consciously and assertively.

Overcoming Gendered Stereotypes in Finance:

The chapter addresses gendered stereotypes that may affect financial decision-making within a matriarchal context. By challenging assumptions about men and women's respective roles in managing money, readers are prompted to break free from limiting stereotypes that may hinder their financial empowerment. This involves recognizing the diversity of financial skills and preferences within both genders, fostering a more inclusive and equitable financial mindset.

Empowering Financial Education:

An essential strategy for navigating matriarchal influences is prioritizing financial education. This section emphasizes the importance of equipping individuals, irrespective of gender, with the knowledge and skills necessary for effective financial decision-making. By fostering financial literacy, individuals can build confidence in making informed choices, thereby countering the impact of matriarchal expectations and assumptions.

Establishing Financial Independence:

The chapter explores the significance of establishing financial independence within the context of matriarchal influences. By encouraging individuals to take ownership of their financial well-being, the focus shifts from reliance on traditional gender roles to fostering autonomy. Strategies for building financial independence include earning, saving, and investing with a focus on personal goals rather than conforming to external expectations.

Negotiating Financial Roles in Relationships:

Navigating matriarchal influences involves negotiating financial roles within relationships. This section provides insights into effective communication about money matters, fostering a collaborative approach to financial decision-making. By openly discussing expectations and responsibilities, individuals can navigate matriarchal influences within partnerships, promoting shared financial goals and mutual empowerment.

Promoting Equal Access to Resources:

The chapter advocates for equal access to financial resources, challenging any disparities influenced by matriarchal expectations. This involves addressing systemic barriers and biases that may limit access to opportunities, resources, and financial education based on gender. By promoting equal access, individuals can work towards dismantling matriarchal influences that perpetuate inequality in financial decision-making.

"Navigating the Matriarchal Influence on Financial Decision-Making: Strategies for Financial Empowerment" serves as a guide for individuals seeking to assert their autonomy and make empowered financial decisions within the context of matriarchal influences. By unpacking matriarchal expectations, challenging gendered stereotypes, prioritizing financial education, establishing financial independence, negotiating roles in relationships, and promoting equal access to resources, individuals can navigate the complexities of matriarchal influences and forge a path towards financial empowerment and independence. This chapter underscores the importance of recognizing and overcoming external influences to shape a financial narrative that aligns with personal goals and values.

CHAPTER FOUR

Balancing Traditional Roles and Financial Autonomy: Overcoming Challenges in a Matriarchal System

Understanding Traditional Gender Roles:

The chapter begins by delving into the historical and cultural underpinnings of traditional gender roles within a matriarchal system. It explores how these roles may influence expectations regarding financial responsibilities, decision-making, and overall financial autonomy. By understanding the roots of these expectations, individuals can better navigate the complexities of traditional roles and work towards reshaping them in a way that aligns with their financial goals.

Fostering Open Communication:

A key strategy for balancing traditional roles and financial autonomy is fostering open and transparent communication within relationships and communities. This involves creating a space where individuals can openly discuss their financial aspirations, concerns, and expectations. By promoting dialogue, individuals can work together to find common ground and negotiate roles that allow for both traditional values and financial independence.

Defying Stereotypes through Action:

Actions often speak louder than words, and this section encourages individuals to defy gender stereotypes through their financial actions. By actively participating in financial decision-making, pursuing career and educational goals, and taking charge of personal finances, individuals can challenge preconceived notions and demonstrate the compatibility of traditional roles with financial autonomy.

Empowering Through Education:

Financial education emerges as a powerful tool in overcoming challenges within a matriarchal system. This involves not only educating oneself but also spreading financial literacy within communities. By empowering individuals with the knowledge and skills necessary for effective financial decision-making, the chapter advocates for a shift towards more informed and autonomous financial practices within the constraints of traditional roles.

Redefining Success and Contribution:

This section explores the importance of redefining success and contribution within the context of a matriarchal system. Rather than adhering strictly to traditional measures of success, individuals are encouraged to define their own paths and contributions. By valuing diverse forms of achievement and financial contribution, individuals can assert their autonomy while respecting the cultural and societal fabric within which they operate.

Collaborative Financial Planning:

Balancing traditional roles and financial autonomy often necessitates collaborative financial planning. This involves working together within families or communities to establish financial goals, allocate resources, and make decisions that align with both traditional expectations and individual aspirations. Collaborative planning fosters a sense of shared responsibility and allows for a more inclusive approach to financial decision-making.

"Balancing Traditional Roles and Financial Autonomy: Overcoming Challenges in a Matriarchal System" serves as a comprehensive guide for individuals navigating the intricate dynamics of traditional gender roles and financial autonomy. By understanding the origins of traditional roles, fostering open communication, defying stereotypes through action, promoting financial education, redefining success, and engaging in collaborative financial planning, individuals can overcome challenges and assert their financial independence within the framework of a matriarchal system. This chapter underscores the importance of finding a harmonious balance between respecting cultural norms and pursuing personal financial empowerment.

CHAPTER FIVE

Navigating Relationship Dynamics and Financial Planning:
Overcoming Challenges in a Matriarchal System

Understanding Relationship Expectations:

The chapter begins by delving into the expectations embedded within relationships in a matriarchal system. Whether familial, spousal, or communal, these expectations often influence financial roles and decision-making. By understanding the nuances of relationship dynamics, individuals can navigate challenges with empathy and open communication, laying the groundwork for more harmonious financial planning.

Promoting Financial Transparency:

A crucial strategy in overcoming challenges within relationship dynamics is fostering financial transparency. This involves open and honest communication about financial goals, aspirations, and challenges. By creating a transparent financial dialogue within relationships, individuals can collectively work towards shared financial objectives while respecting the cultural and societal expectations that shape their dynamics.

Establishing Shared Financial Goals:

Collaborative financial goal-setting emerges as a key component in navigating relationship dynamics. This section encourages individuals to engage in a dialogue with their partners or family members to establish shared financial goals. By aligning aspirations and priorities, individuals can foster a sense of unity and mutual understanding, creating a foundation for financial planning that respects both personal autonomy and communal expectations.

Negotiating Financial Responsibilities:

Within a matriarchal system, traditional expectations often assign specific financial responsibilities to individuals based on their roles within relationships. This part of the chapter explores the importance of negotiating these responsibilities to ensure fairness and equity. By openly discussing and redefining financial roles, individuals can navigate challenges and establish a balance that respects both tradition and financial autonomy.

Encouraging Joint Financial Planning:

Joint financial planning is advocated as a proactive strategy for navigating relationship dynamics. This involves actively involving all parties in financial decision-making processes, fostering a collaborative approach to financial planning. By encouraging joint involvement, individuals can overcome challenges and work towards financial goals that are collectively established and mutually beneficial.

Embracing Individual Financial Independence:

While navigating relationship dynamics, the chapter also underscores the significance of embracing individual financial independence. This involves recognizing the importance of personal financial goals and autonomy within the context of relationships. By balancing communal expectations with personal aspirations, individuals can assert their financial independence without compromising the integrity of their relationships.

Conclusion:

"Navigating Relationship Dynamics and Financial Planning: Overcoming Challenges in a Matriarchal System" serves as a comprehensive guide for individuals seeking to navigate the complex interplay between relationships and financial decisions within a matriarchal context. By understanding relationship expectations, promoting financial transparency, establishing shared financial goals, negotiating responsibilities, encouraging joint financial planning, and embracing individual financial independence, individuals can overcome challenges and create a harmonious balance between personal autonomy and cultural expectations. This chapter highlights the importance of fostering open communication, empathy, and collaboration to achieve financial well-being while respecting the dynamics of relationships within a matriarchal system.

The Power of Vision:

This section delves into the concept of vision and its profound impact on life's trajectory. A vision acts as a compass, providing direction and purpose. It goes beyond mere goal-setting by encapsulating a holistic image of the life one desires. By acknowledging the power of vision, individuals can tap into a wellspring of motivation and clarity, laying the foundation for intentional and purpose-driven living.

Reflecting on Core Values:

Creating a vision for your ideal life begins with a deep reflection on core values. This involves identifying the principles and beliefs that are fundamental to your sense of self and fulfillment. By aligning your vision with your core values, you ensure that your aspirations are authentic and resonate with the essence of who you are.

Visualizing Specific Goals:

The chapter emphasizes the importance of translating your vision into specific, actionable goals. Visualization is a powerful tool in this process, allowing individuals to vividly picture the outcomes they desire. By breaking down the overarching vision into concrete, achievable goals, individuals can create a roadmap for progress and celebrate the incremental steps toward their ideal life.

Balancing Professional and Personal Aspirations:

Crafting a life, you love involves striking a balance between professional and personal aspirations. This section explores the integration of career goals with personal values and lifestyle choices. By aligning professional pursuits with the broader vision for an ideal life, individuals can foster a sense of harmony and satisfaction across all facets of their existence.

Embracing Adaptability and Resilience:

The journey towards an ideal life is seldom a linear path. Challenges, setbacks, and unexpected changes are inevitable. This part of the chapter encourages individuals to embrace adaptability and resilience as integral components of the vision-building process. By viewing obstacles as opportunities for growth, individuals can navigate the inevitable twists and turns with grace and determination.

Implementing Daily Practices:

Creating a vision for your ideal life requires consistent and intentional action. This section explores the importance of daily practices that align with your vision. Whether it's cultivating healthy habits, nurturing relationships, or pursuing personal and professional development, these practices serve as the building blocks for crafting a life that reflects your ideals.

Cultivating Gratitude and Reflection:

Gratitude and reflection play a pivotal role in the journey towards an ideal life. This segment encourages individuals to regularly acknowledge and appreciate the progress made, fostering a positive mindset. By cultivating gratitude for the present moment and reflecting on the journey, individuals can stay connected to their vision while appreciating the richness of their evolving lives.

Conclusion:

"Creating a Vision for Your Ideal Life: Crafting a Life You Love" serves as a roadmap for individuals seeking to transform their aspirations into reality. By understanding the power of vision, reflecting on core values, visualizing specific goals, balancing professional and personal aspirations, embracing adaptability, implementing daily practices, and cultivating gratitude and reflection, individuals can embark on a purposeful and fulfilling journey toward a life they genuinely love. This chapter underscores the transformative potential of envisioning an ideal life and actively participating in the ongoing process of crafting a life that aligns with personal values, passions, and aspirations.

Embracing Financial Freedom: A Journey to Empowerment

Redefining Financial Freedom:

At its core, financial freedom is not merely about accumulating wealth; it is about redefining the very concept of freedom. It involves liberating oneself from the shackles of financial stress, cultivating a healthy relationship with money, and empowering individuals to make choices that align with their values and long-term goals. This redefinition underscores the holistic nature of financial freedom—a freedom that extends beyond monetary constraints to encompass emotional well-being and personal fulfillment.

The Role of Mindset in Financial Liberation:

Throughout our exploration, the pivotal role of mindset in achieving financial freedom has emerged as a recurring theme. Shifting from a scarcity mindset to an abundance mindset, overcoming limiting beliefs, and fostering a positive money mindset are foundational steps in this journey. The conclusion reaffirms that true financial freedom is not solely an external pursuit but a deeply internal one—a transformation of beliefs and attitudes that paves the way for sustainable financial empowerment.

Balancing Tradition and Autonomy:

In the context of diverse societal structures, our exploration has highlighted the delicate dance between tradition and individual autonomy. Whether navigating matriarchal influences, challenging stereotypes, or balancing traditional roles with financial independence, the conclusion underscores the importance of finding a harmonious balance. It advocates for the empowerment that comes from embracing tradition while asserting one's autonomy in financial decision-making, thereby creating a path to genuine freedom.

Crafting a Vision for a Life You Love:

The journey towards financial freedom culminates in the crafting of a vision for a life that resonates with personal values and aspirations. This conclusion emphasizes the transformative power of envisioning one's ideal life and actively working towards it. By aligning financial goals with core values, individuals can create a roadmap for a purpose-driven life—one filled with passion, joy, and a sense of fulfillment.

Empowering Through Financial Education:

A cornerstone of financial freedom is empowerment through education. The conclusion reiterates the significance of financial literacy as a tool for breaking free from the cycles of financial insecurity. By equipping individuals with the knowledge and skills necessary for sound financial decision-making, financial education becomes a catalyst for empowerment, fostering a sense of control over one's financial destiny.

Cultivating Resilience and Gratitude:

The journey towards financial freedom is not without its challenges, and the conclusion emphasizes the importance of cultivating resilience and gratitude along the way. Embracing setbacks as opportunities for growth, staying adaptable in the face of change, and fostering a mindset of gratitude contribute to a resilient and empowered approach to financial freedom.

Conclusion:

In concluding the exploration of "Embracing Financial Freedom," it becomes evident that this journey is a profound and multifaceted endeavor. It encompasses the redefinition of freedom, the transformative power of mindset shifts, the delicate balance between tradition and autonomy, the crafting of a vision for a life one loves, the empowerment through financial education, and the cultivation of resilience and gratitude. Financial freedom is not a destination but a continuous journey—a journey that empowers individuals to shape their lives in alignment with their values, aspirations, and dreams. As we embrace financial freedom, we embark on a path of self-discovery, empowerment, and the creation of a life that reflects the true essence of freedom and fulfillment.